The Unworthy

The Unworthy

A Blue Collar Approach To Fixing
Americas Economy

Blue Collar Economist

Copyright © 2012 by Blue Collar Economist.

Library of Congress Control Number: 2012900248
ISBN: Hardcover   978-1-4691-4695-9
              Softcover   978-1-4691-4694-2
              Ebook   978-1-4691-4696-6

All rights reserved. No part of this book may be reproduced or transmitted in any form or by any means, electronic or mechanical, including photocopying, recording, or by any information storage and retrieval system, without permission in writing from the copyright owner.

This book was printed in the United States of America.

To order additional copies of this book, contact:
Xlibris Corporation
1-888-795-4274
www.Xlibris.com
Orders@Xlibris.com

Contents

Prologue 9

Who Is Responsible for America's Present Economic Situation? 17

The American Dream, but Not in America 28

Why Universal Health 39

My Personal Experience as a Patient with
    the American Health-Care System 48

I want to dedicate this book to all working people: blue-collar, white-collar, working poor, veterans, and students and also to the underprivileged, disabled, and people born into poverty. The American labor movement, a movement that has made life better for all Americans by fighting for the forty-hour workweek, weekends, national holidays, overtime pay, health care, and retirement benefits. But especially I want to dedicate this book to Occupy Wall Street. Those brave, noble souls that, in the tradition of the civil rights movement, have the guts to stand up for the rights of all Americans in peaceful protest.

PROLOGUE

I am the Blue-Collar Economist, and my goal is to educate the American people and businessmen about the economy, the policies, and the people that caused America's current difficult economic situation and the changes to those policies we must make as a nation to become a prosperous, humane nation again in simple blue-collar language that even a five-year-old can understand. I will also repeat some of the same facts over and over again in different ways to emphasize their importance.

If you read nothing but this prologue, you will know the simple techniques the powerful elite used, and always use, to scam you, the public, out of your hard-earned money; approximately what our current economic situation is; and what we must do to reverse the economic and social damage that has been done over the past thirty years of neocon policies and reestablish ourselves as a prosperous and humane society. Of course, I would like you to read my whole book, but even if you don't, the prologue will explain the basic concepts.

The economy in many ways is like a football, baseball, or basketball game: there is competition, competing parties (teams), winners, and losers, and there will always be a small percentage of greedy, highly dysfunctional individuals who will do anything to win. In sports and in economies, there have to be rules to play by and referees to enforce those rules. The problem with America is that in the last thirty years, the powerful and greedy few have corrupted the system, eliminated the rules, and bribed the referees.

In America, it is easy to pick out the competing teams; the visiting team is the 99 percent, which I will call the Ninetyniners, and the home team is the 1 percent, which I will call TheElitists. I will make Elizabeth Warren the coach of the Ninetyniners and the Koch brothers the coach of TheElitists. Appropriate, don't you think?

If the game were being held over thirty years ago, the game wouldn't be quite so lopsided because the average CEO only made thirty times what the average worker made, and there were good banking regulations preventing corrupt politicians, bankers, and brokers from robbing the populace blind. Now the average CEO makes three hundred times what the average worker makes, and there are no rules governing corruption in the government or the financial sector. The rules for banking and Wall Street started to be eliminated during the Reagan administration and continued with a feverish pace for the next thirty years, which along with massive overspending on defense, massive decreases in taxes for the very rich, and continued control of the health-care industry by the greedy CEOs of insurance, pharmacy, and hospital corporations, has resulted in a massive financial mismatch between the 99 percent and the 1 percent.

In the past thirty years there have been no rules, except the rules that favor the 1 percent, and no honest referees because the politicians, the judicial system, and the regulatory agencies have all been corrupted by the 1 percent. To illustrate this, consider this: the forty years prior to the Reagan administration, when deregulation started, America had no major financial crisis. But after deregulation was started by Reagan, we've had one financial crisis right after another: the savings and loan collapse, the Enron Debacle, the mortgage loan crisis, and the Wall Street financial crisis; and although every one of those crises were created by the elite ruling class of America, you, the working-class taxpayer, got stuck with $15 trillion bill (that's $60,000 of debt for every working man, woman, and child in America) while the ruling elite have grown their wealth by 300 percent and own close to 50 percent of everything in America even though they only make up 1 percent.

Let's review. In the last thirty years, a grotesquely greedy and disturbingly dysfunctional but small portion of American society (people like the Bushes, the Murdochs, the Koch brothers, etc.) used their political influence and wealth to game the system, to eliminate or change the rules, and to corrupt the referees and some of the opposing players to create an unfair advantage for their team, TheElitists. They had the rules that kept the game fair completely eliminated, like the Glass-Steagall Banking Act, which was put in place to protect the American people from unfair banking practices (like letting corrupt bankers invest depositor money in high-risk investments), or other rules meant to protect Americans from similar abuses by the savings and loan industry, the mortgage industry, and Wall Street. Then they instituted new rules that effectively guaranteed they would win 100 percent of the time, like the Commodities Futures Modernization Act, which effectively allowed Wall Street to rob the US Treasury and the American taxpayer of trillions of dollars, so there were no rules anymore to protect the average citizen or businessman in America. Then they set about corrupting our referees: our politicians (the White House, the Senate, Congress, the secretary treasurer [Alan Greenspan, Hank Paulson]), our judicial system (the Supreme Court, the US Attorney, district attorneys, state and local judges), our regulatory agencies (the Securities and Exchange Commission), and our rating agencies (Moody's and Standard & Poor's) with—yes, you guessed it—money. And just to make sure it isn't easy to change the rules back to the old fair rules that existed prior to Reagan, they are making it more difficult to vote with draconian voting regulations, another way of rigging the system in their favor. So the Great Depression of 1929 and our recent financial crisis were all caused by exactly the same policies: deregulation of the financial sector and undertaxation of the megarich. Today the game is being rigged completely in favor of the 1 percent, making it close to impossible for the poor and lower-middle-class person to achieve the American dream.

Now I am going list the steps we need to take as a Nation, to recreate the country America was in the '50s, '60s, and '70s, minus the Vietnam War, with greater economic growth, low unemployment, an equally low cost of education, massive growth in the middle class, and middle class wealth. By the way, don't let any of your boneheaded, corrupt politicians convince you that any of these steps are not necessary—they're idiots.

1. Reduce defense spending to 10 percent of GDP from its present level of 20 percent of GDP. This will save at least $400 billion annually. We can use that money to create jobs and innovation in the private sector, like bullet trains, wind energy, and solar energy technology.
2. We must return to a progressive tax rate for everybody. Clinton-era taxes are a good start. This will save $700 billion annually. Remember, the United States is running about a $1.25 trillion to $1.5 trillion deficit annually; $700 billion would take care of half to two-thirds of that annual debt. The return to Clinton-era taxes for the middle class will not hurt the middle class because, as you will see, there will be much bigger savings for them through reducing health-care costs and reestablishing full employment.
3. Make sure we establish strong laws to regulate the financial sector (banks and Wall Street) and make sure our regulatory agencies are given the tools they need to enforce those regulations and that they are not corrupted by money. Remember, the deregulation starting with the Reagan administration and continuing with Bush II has been the cause for every one of our financial crisis of the last thirty years at a cost of $15 trillion-$20 trillion dollars of taxpayer debt that would not have occurred had it not been for deregulation. It is also the major reason for the massive transfer of wealth from the working man to the 1 percent.
4. We must extend the payroll tax to the first $200,000 of income instead of just the first $106,000 of income to stabilize our system of social security for the foreseeable future. We must also make laws to prevent creepy politicians from robbing the social security fund to fight unjustified wars of occupation.
5. Capital gains should be taxed at the same rate as income after the first $100,000. It is ridiculous that people born into wealth

and privilege, like Bush and Romney, who make most of their income from capital gains, pay half the taxes that a hardworking blue-collar worker pays. When they are just sitting back and letting their financial advisers make massive amounts of money for them while they live in a permanent state of retirement. Right now in America, privilege is valued over work.

6. The over-the-counter-derivatives market that helped get our country and the world into the financial mess it is in today should have a transaction tax placed on it of least a fourth of a percent per transaction.
7. Social Security should be means tested as a way of assuring our social security system is well funded and prosperous. Wealthy people don't need the degree of social security support that poor and disabled people do.
8. We need to outlaw the credit default swap (CDS), a transaction that is essentially an illegal bet on the market that only brokers, with inside information, and their clients benefit from and that no politician would allow unless they have been totally corrupted by big money from Wall Street (like Phil Graham and his wife).
9. We need to change the senate rules that require a 60 percent majority to pass any legislation to a simple majority of 51 percent because the current rule has paralyzed our political system so that nothing gets done anymore except senators getting immensely rich, taking bribes to tactically obstruct the process on behalf of powerful special interests.
10. Reverse the *Citizens United* decision made by the most partisan and corrupt Supreme Court in over fifty years. Once again, like all Repub neocon policies, it is aimed at taking away what little say the working man has in his own government.
11. We need to establish a really good recycling system like Germany's. We are the most wasteful society in history, and there are many spin-off businesses that could be spurred by a progressive recycling program.

12. And finally, the most important change of all: America must switch from our outdated, massively overexpensive, unfairly distributed health-care system to one exactly like the best health-care system in the world, Taiwan's.

These changes will accomplish the following: pay off our $15 trillion-$16 trillion debt in a decade, create full employment, reduce the fifty thousand Americans that die annually because they can't access health care to zero, reduce the one million people who go bankrupt every year in America because of health-care costs to zero, reduce our present poverty rate of 16 percent to almost zero, increase our economic growth from almost zero to 6 to 10 percent of GDP annually, reestablish fair elections, reduce the disparity between rich and poor, and reestablish the value of work over privilege. As a bonus, our politicians will become much less corrupt.

I also want to dispel a few neocon myths: (1) Immigrants have nothing to do with our present economic situation; quite the opposite, they provide reliable inexpensive labor and they pay taxes and ultimately become a valuable part of the fabric and culture of America. (2) Reducing what we spend on defense will not affect our security in any way; it will just make it much more focused and effective. (3) We should welcome freedom of choice, a woman's right to choose, and religious freedom. It is what our nation was built on despite what Reverend Hagee and other crazy nuts like him say to the contrary. (4) Labor unions are the most valuable working man's advocate, and letting boneheads like Governor Walker of Wisconsin and others like him convince you otherwise is like being convinced that it is in your best interest to jump into a pool of sulfuric acid. (5) There is no such thing as trickle-down economics; in fact, that myth has done more to destroy our democracy than any other of the crazy myths propagated by Fox News and friends. (6) We shouldn't privatize social security and Medicare. The only changes we should make is to switch to a universal health-care system, like Taiwan's, and extend the payroll tax to the first $200,000 of income. (7) The claim that universal health care would take away the patient's ability to choose their own doctor and force them to buy insurance, which they say is unconstitutional, is a myth created by individuals who know absolutely nothing about health care and have a vested interest in keeping the system the way it is. The truth is that universal health care would guarantee you that you could keep your own doctor, would improve the quality of health care many times over, would eliminate the gatekeeper system, virtually eliminate paperwork, cost half as much, and save our Medicare and Medicaid system financially for the foreseeable future, eliminating it as a political issue. It would eliminate any attempt to get rid of or change Medicare or Medicaid. (8) That we should profile Muslims or that American Muslims pose any threat to America. Only somebody as incredibly stupid as Rick Santorum or Herman Cain would propose such a ridiculous idea. Pinheads.

Finally, I want to emphasize the importance of voting. If we had not voted Reagan and Bush II into office, we would not be in the despairing economic situation we are in today, and we wouldn't have been talked into two unfunded and useless wars. We as a people must show more discretion when we enter the voting booth. Presently, I wouldn't vote for a single Republican or Blue Dog Democrat; they certainly were to a large degree to blame for our present situation.

WHO IS RESPONSIBLE FOR AMERICA'S PRESENT ECONOMIC SITUATION?

I am going to describe a group of people to you because it is vital that you understand who these people are since they frequently end up controlling our government, the media, our financial markets, our legal system, and even our military and secret service, which they have often used to protect their own foreign assets and to acquire new assets in foreign lands, both for themselves and their good old boy network of friends. Just as important is the fact that they have access to the US Treasury, which I will call the People's Bank Account. The US Treasury is the accumulated wealth or debt of working people, where money is deposited through taxation or withdrawn to pay the country's bills. Unfortunately for you, once your tax dollars are deposited into the US Treasury, the Congress, under the influence of the president and hundreds of special-interest lobbyists, control the purse strings to your account. Of course, you and I don't have lobbyists to represent us, nor do we have any way of protecting our money once it has been collected by the government. Thus, it becomes easy pickings for corrupt politicians and the individuals and companies who control them. The only way the people of America can prevent what has happened over the past thirty years is by voting politicians into office who aren't corrupt. But unfortunately for Americans, in the last thirty years starting with Reagan, their votes have done more harm to themselves and the nation than good. It has taken very little effort on the part of greedy industrialists, like the Koch brothers, and media moguls, like Lester Murdoch, to hoodwink voters into voting for bought, corrupted politicians who happily vote for legislation that favors the CEOs of the military-industrial complex, Wall Street, the health-care industry, and others who have robbed the US Treasury of three generations of taxpayer wealth. They did it the same way dictators, tyrants, royal families, and the ruling elite, of all countries, have done it for eons. They used simple, mindless propaganda, repeating the same talking points over and over again—if you say it enough times, it becomes the truth—and tying it to patriotism, God, and the hysterical fear of a trumped-up enemy. It almost always works, and they know it. And of course, the underlying goal behind these propaganda campaigns is to divide and distract the populace so the foxes can rob the chicken coop. It's that simple

So to be brutally honest with you, in the last thirty years, politicians, mortgage loan companies, bankers, Wall Street brokers, hedge fund managers, pharmaceutical companies, hospital corporations, health insurance companies, lobbyists, defense contractors, and oil companies have all joined in the feeding frenzy of greed, all finding ways to milk the American taxpayer and drain the US Treasury. Yes, putting your money under the stewardship of our government has been like leaving the foxes in charge of the chicken coop. But you know, a farmer or rancher would never let his chicken coop be Robbed so many times without making some effort to protect it.

In other words, over the last thirty years the American voter just kept leaving the same nasty old foxes to guard the chicken coop over and over again, resulting in massive amounts of debt equaling $60,000 for every working man, woman, and child in America. And who were the worst of the foxes guarding the chicken coop? That is easy to answer. The facts are undeniable; the Republican administrations are by far the worst of the nasty old foxes guarding the chicken coop, but that doesn't mean that Democrats don't have some culpability. The basic policies of the Republicans and now the Tea Party are simple: war for profit, social conservatism, deregulation, and lower the taxes for the "Job Creators." In plain English, they are chicken hawkery, xenophobia, religious fanaticism, and greed. The need to start wars for profit gave us three unjustified wars: Vietnam, Iraq, and Afghanistan, with the Iraq and Afghanistan wars being unfunded, which Joseph Stiglitz, a Nobel Prize-winning economist, said will ultimately cost Americans $5 trillion-6 trillion. Deregulation, which began with Reagan, was the cause of the savings and loan collapse, the Enron Debacle, the subprime mortgage crisis, and the collapse of Wall Street; total cost, maybe $14 trillion-$15 trillion.

The lies of Grover Norquist and others caused Republican politicians and Blue Dog Democrats, scared stiff to break the Grover Norquist pledge, not to raise taxes and instead to actually lower the taxes of the very rich to an effective tax rate of 15 percent because many of the very rich make all their income on investments and can therefore call their income capital gains. This cost the country a cool $7 trillion over the last decade, making it impossible for the country to pay its bills, thus racking up massive debts for future generations of working Americans to pay. The lies that kept us from adopting universal health care came from the Fox noise machine and politicians corrupted by the money from Big Pharma, hospital corporations, and insurance corporations that is costing the American people $1.25 trillion annually.

The total cost of unfunded wars, deregulation, private-insurance-run health care, and undertaxation over the past thirty years is certainly in the twenties of trillions of dollars. Remember, at the end of the Carter administration the country only had a debt of about $2 trillion, and the Clinton administration essentially didn't add much to that. But with Reagan and the beginning of deregulation, his administration added something like $3 trillion to the federal debt, more than doubling the existing national debt. And then Bush and Cheney essentially added another $10 trillion to the debt, which now stands at almost $15 trillion, almost eight times the debt as was created in the previous two hundred years of our history in just thirty years, and most of it in just the eight years of the Bush/Cheney administration. You can quibble about the Obama administration's contribution, but whatever has been added to the national debt during his administration was required in order to bail us out of the horrendous financial mess Bush and Cheney got us into, and of course, Obama had no choice but to continue the Bush tax cuts and the two unfunded and purposeless wars. But that isn't the full accounting of the debt created by the Bush and Cheney administration because during the same period the nation was neglecting repairing and replacing its infrastructure, which in many cases is now so dilapidated as to be unsafe. I call this the accumulated infrastructure debt of the Bush/Cheney administration; and added into the ongoing cost of their two unfunded wars, the ongoing cost of the Bush tax cuts, the unfunded Medicare part D supplement, the cost of the financial crises (both mortgage and Wall Street) because of deregulation, I am going to say the total cost of the Bush/Cheney administration is in the twenties of trillions of dollars. That's what I call balancing the budget.

I think it is safe to say that Bush and Cheney needlessly squandered the taxes of the next two or three generations of working people. How did two little innocuous, nefarious little guys cause so much damage in such a short time? Why did you vote for people like Nixon, Reagan, and Bush, and Cheney, and why would you be thinking about voting for someone just like them again? There are many reasons, and I will discuss them later in the book.

Whatever the reasons, the politicians I mentioned took full advantage of your trust to enrich themselves and their cronies at your expense. They used the media, mainly Fox News, but also the other major networks, to brainwash and con you. They used the Pentagon and your tax dollars to train a group of retired generals, who were all financially tied to the arms industry as consultants and lobbyists, in talking points to promote the war. The very same talking points that (Bring 'Em On) Bush, (Debt Doesn't Matter) Cheney, (I Believe My Own Lies) Rice, (I Didn't Know I Was Lying to the UN) Powell, and (The Grim Reaper) Rumsfield were using. The question is, what can we do in the future to avoid these catastrophic voting mistakes? We can't go back in time and reverse history, and we can't correct the mistakes we have already made, and we can't recover the more than $15 trillion of taxpayer money that was robbed from the US Treasury, money that was already transferred to the offshore tax-free accounts of the CEOs, bankers, and brokers who legally stole it. It's spilled milk, water under the bridge, and the train that's already left the station; $15 trillion gone and counting. We, the public, must educate ourselves about the issues, the candidates, and some basic economics. I will help you with the economics and make it so simple that even a five-year-old can understand it. Voting is the one little bit of leverage the average working stiff has in this country, so we have to stop wasting our vote on corrupt politicians or there won't be an American dream for future generations of working kids. By the way, getting your information from Fox News is the opposite of educating yourself.

Let me elaborate on just how big the wound is to our country as a result of voting George Bush and Dick Cheney into office. To put it into perspective, it is very possible that if we had not voted for George Bush and Dick Cheney, our nation's status would be as follows: (1) Our annual budgets would have been balanced in the past ten years instead of running trillion-dollar annual deficits. (2) Our total national debt would only be about $3 trillion instead our present debt of $15 trillion and growing. (3) I don't have any doubt we would have full employment, meaning 3-4 percent instead of our present level of 9-11 percent. (4) We wouldn't have been conned into two unjustified and unfunded wars, and 100,000 innocent Iraqi and Afghan women and children would still be alive, tens of millions of Iraqi and Afghan citizens wouldn't have been displaced as refugees, 4,500 American soldiers would still be alive, and 30,000 wouldn't have been wounded or disabled. (5) I think we would have universal health care by now, which I can guarantee you as a doctor would be many times better than the health-care system we have, which is rated the worst in the developed world (number 37) and the most expensive, costing twice as much per capita as other health-care systems. Think about it, Americans and American businesses would save 50 percent of the cost of health care as would the federal government and retired people on Medicare. That savings would immediately lower the cost of manufacturing and put lots more money back in the pockets of private citizens, creating millions of new manufacturing and service jobs, and in addition, because our health-care industry would once again be the best in the world at a reasonable price, it would create millions more jobs in the health industry because of increases in both American patients and foreign patients.

Get the picture? No savings and loan collapse; no Enron; no mortgage loan crisis; no Wall Street crisis; no worldwide financial crisis caused by unregulated financial institutions and Wall Street bankers and brokers; forty-six million Americans wouldn't be living in poverty (twenty-two million of those children); fifty million Americans wouldn't be without health insurance; another one hundred million Americans wouldn't be underinsured; one million Americans wouldn't be going bankrupt each year because of overwhelming health-care expenses; fifty thousand Americans wouldn't die needlessly every year because of poor or no access to health care; the cost of college would be affordable by all, not just the elite ruling class; working-class children wouldn't be in hock for the rest of their lives for the cost of a secondary education; and tens of millions of Americans wouldn't have lost their homes, their pensions, their savings, and in many cases their lives and their futures if we just hadn't elected Nixon, Reagan, Bush II, and Cheney. It's the America that could have been and the American voter's road not taken. Again you have to live in amazement of what two fairly little, innocuous guys, with a little help from Reagan, did in just eight years. However, they didn't work alone.

If a certain class of people weren't born with such power and wealth, virtually none of the events of the past thirty years could have happened. They are the elite ruling class, like the Bushes, Dulles, Romneys, and Kennedys. Not all of them are dysfunctional, greedy, and desperate for more money and power, but many are. They are almost always responsible for unjustified wars of occupation and economic policies that cause unfair disparities in wealth, which result in massive poverty and inequality. Oftentimes, they are even able to co-opt large numbers of the working class to support their draconian policies using dog whistles like patriotism, religion, fear, and trumped-up villains when, in fact, they are the real villains.

In America the disparity between the rich (who are doubling their wealth every decade on average) and the poor and middle class (who haven't increased their wealth one penny in over thirty years) is the second worst in the developed world. To quote one of the wealthiest men in America, Warren Buffett, "The rich are literally drowning in wealth," and, "I am one of the richest men in America and I pay a lower effective tax rate than my secretary." Another great American, Charles Barkley, put it even more simply, "America has become the place where the rich screw the poor."

While the great American middle class hasn't made a single gain in income or wealth in the last thirty years and is oftentimes drowning in debt, the rich are getting richer at a culturally obscene rate. The individual who through no fault of their own but simply out of the pure dumb luck of being born into abject wealth and privilege (Bush and Romney) will experience only the best of what America has to offer: the best schools, most opportunity, lavish vacations, absolute financial security, and a wealthy network of (good old boy) friends and financial advisers (already set up by their parents) to make sure they always are guaranteed a spot at the front of the line in life and in business. If life were a race to reach the top of a ladder, these kids just skip the race; Mom and Dad gently place them on the top of the ladder, present them with a blue ribbon, and give them a big victory smooch. In other words, they have few hurdles to overcome, have very few obstacles, and will never have to compete in life without the game being rigged in their favor. Thus, they enter life with an air of confidence, usually verging on arrogance, which—along with the riches they own and power they wield—succinctly and unmistakenly separates them from us, the working class. What they rarely realize is that they are the recipients of the purest form of social welfare, the pure dumb luck of birthright, and in fact, they often feel strongly that they not only deserve everything they have inherited by virtue of pedigree or divine providence but that others, who are less fortunate, also deserve what they have inherited.

George Bush Jr. is the best example of the people I have just described. George made his fortune, in addition to the one he inherited, by using the leverage Daddy's (good-old-boy) network provided to him. In this case, George Sr.'s (good-old-boy) network found a lucrative scam for both themselves and little George. They knew the owners of the Texas Rangers were ready to sell the franchise and sell it cheap. They knew all about a successful scam that the owners of other professional sports franchises had already worked out. The scam goes something like this: find a corrupt politician and pay him to float a bond issue so taxpayers agree to pay for a new stadium, disguise it as something else on the ballot, make sure the bond issue gives ownership of the stadium, and the right to sell it, to the new franchise owners, not to the tax payers who actually purchased it and should have owned it. You can guess the rest. George and his crooked partners made a cool $20 million apiece in profit from selling the new stadium, which the taxpayers bought for them. Then just to rub salt into the wound, George and his partners only paid 15 percent tax on the income instead of 39 percent because they claimed it as capital gains instead of income. Not bad, wouldn't you say? I've heard that Texans used to hang men for stealing a couple of horses, but with George and his (good-old-boy) business partners, Texans literally thanked them for the privilege of being fleeced. Huh, huh, my name is George Bush, and I want to thank you kindly.

Well, you can see that George and his partners didn't have to come up with some brilliant plan to fleece the taxpayers of Texas. They simply needed to be born into abject wealth and power so they or their powerful parents could politically influence or corrupt a politician or two. The voters were defenseless; they never knew what happened because it was all done without their knowledge and, likewise, so are all the scams that were pulled off by corrupt politicians, bankers, Wall Street brokers, and lobbyists that ended up draining the US Treasury during the Bush/

Cheney era. Wall Street use of the "over the counter" unregulated securities market (a market deregulated by corrupt politicians like Phil Graham and his wife, surprise!), and once that was taken care of, the scam was simple: use your political influence and money to corrupt the Securities Exchange Commission, the agency that is supposed to regulate the derivatives market, and the two rating companies (Standard & Poor's and Moody's) who agreed to rate the toxic mortgage-backed securities or derivatives triple A when they knew they weren't even double C. There were so many ways to make money on this scam that the piranhas on Wall Street and in the banks were literally tripping over each other to see who could be the greediest. First, there was the hundreds of billions of dollars in brokers commissions to be made. Second, brokers and bankers who had inside information and enough money could buy a sure bet called a credit default swap (CDS), which was a legal bet that the derivative would default and, of course; they already knew it was going to default and would pay the broker the full value of the derivative even though they weren't the owner of the derivative. The crazy thing is that the financial firms (bookies) that sold the credit default swaps (bets) didn't have the money to cover them when they came due. Well, that's all right because they knew that you, the taxpayer, would cover them, and you did, for hundreds of billions of dollars. Of course, it wasn't exactly you who decided to cover those bad bets. It was really Hank Paulson, President Bush, the Congress, the Senate, and President Obama, but you don't really mind, do you? Oh yes, and good old Alan Greenspan was very diligent about looking the other way while all this was happening—always a good soldier.

The Iraq War was also a simple scam to set up: just corrupt CIA director George Tenet what's to corrupt (remember the "it's a slam dunk to sell the war" comment?); get the secretary of defense, General Powell, to go along with the charade (also not that difficult); corrupt enough senators and congressmen (extremely easy, even Hillary went along with it); bribe a pathologic liar named Curve Ball to say he was a former colonel in the Iraqi army and that Al Qaeda was plotting with Saddam; and have Mr.

Tony Blair and his corrupt security chief falsely legitimize Curve Balls Story and create a little Chicken-Little-the-sky-is-falling-in hysteria, and it was done. I could tell by the look on his face that even George W. Bush was surprised by how slick and easy the whole scam turned out to be, like a hot knife through butter.

The subprime mortgage debacle was exactly the same process as all your basic Washington scams. The use of power, money, and influence to deregulate, corrupt, and pay; a little propaganda is sometimes required also. The great thing is that nobody is ever prosecuted because even though a five-year-old can understand what happened, and the politicians themselves have some significant culpability, they tell the public it is all too complex for them to understand; therefore, they can't figure out where to place the blame.

In all these scams, the goal was simple, which was to rob hundreds of billions of dollars of hard-earned taxpayer money from the US Treasury and transfer it to the offshore tax-free accounts of the scammers, who did nothing productive but use their influence and money to corrupt the system and pull off a simple scam. The only way that we, the public, can prevent these scams is to not fall prey to the simple techniques that are always used to pull them off. The scammers always associate themselves and their cause with patriotism, Christianity (in America), fear of a trumped-up enemy that they are going to save you from (and that enemy could be anybody: the unions, Muslims, government workers, the poor, poor children, Occupy Wall Street, Iran, immigrants, anybody who just wants to vote, anybody who doesn't believe in condoning everything that the present Israeli government does, anybody who wants a fair tax code, anybody who wants to reduce defense spending, anybody who wants a really good health-care system, anybody who believes in a woman's right to choose, etc.). Here, I am making this too complex. What they are doing is called divide and conquer. Why do you think the stinky little Koch brothers fund any movement or institution (the Tea Party, the Heritage Foundation, Cato Institute, Americans for Prosperity, etc.) that divides working people from each other? They are far from the brightest bulbs on the tree, but they know what all individuals born into privilege and wealth know—that propaganda works.

The bottom line is this, the very small elite ruling class doesn't comprise a significant portion of our population, but because they control so much of our society—government, media, the military, and the Secret Service, most of the land resources, property, and wealth—we, the people, need to be especially vigilant not to let them influence us to the point that we work against each other and lose what little leverage we have.

THE AMERICAN DREAM, BUT NOT IN AMERICA

People, here is the simple truth about America: We have almost fifty million Americans living below the poverty line, which includes twenty-two million children. We have fifty million Americans uninsured and another one hundred million Americans underinsured, resulting in fifty thousand needless deaths every year due to lack of access to health care, and one million Americans who have to file bankruptcy annually because of excessive health-care costs. We have a real unemployment rate of 9-12 percent and a dangerous level of national debt, created by corrupt politicians who used the US Treasury like an open-ended credit card and ran up a bill equal to $60,000 for every man, woman, and child in America. A debt that is destroying the American dream. A debt that is the major reason for the low academic standing of American students in math and science; the reason we have the worst disparity between rich and poor in the developed world; the reason the safety net that previous generations created for seniors, the disabled, and working poor is also being stolen right from under their noses by the very same corrupt politicians, Wall Street bankers, and brokers; and the reason America is experiencing virtually no economic growth and inadequate new jobs. Why has this happened?

Before I get to the reasons why we find ourselves in this situation, a situation that is potentially going to get much worse in the coming years unless America makes some basic economic and legal changes, I want to describe a country that has achieved the American dream and how they did it.

Taiwan is a small country that is part of China but is governed independently. Let's compare the economic and social situation of Taiwan to that of the United States and then try to ascertain the reasons there is such disparity in the level of general well-being, prosperity, and economic stability.

Taiwan only has about 1 percent of its population that lives in poverty versus America, which has about 16 percent. Taiwan only has about 3-4 percent unemployment versus America, which has somewhere between 10 and 16 percent real unemployment. Taiwan's economy is growing at a rate of 4-8 percent of its GDP annually versus America, which isn't growing its GDP at all. Taiwan only has a debt of 36 percent of its GDP versus the United States, which has a crippling debt of 110 percent of its GDP. Taiwan doesn't have anybody without good health insurance, and absolutely nobody goes bankrupt due to health-care expenses versus America, which has fifty million people without health insurance, plus another one hundred million who are underinsured, and one million people that go bankrupt every year due to health-care expenses, 45 percent of whom actually had health insurance. Taiwan only spends 8 percent of its GDP on health care and probably has the best health-care system in the developed world versus the United States, which is spending in excess of 17.5 percent of its GDP on health care and is rated number 37 by the World Health Organization (WHO), the worst in the developed world. Taiwan's students routinely score in the top three in math and science, and secondary education is virtually free, versus America's students who rate somewhere between 20 and 25 in math and science and where the cost of education is beyond the reach of many, if not most, working-class students. Taiwan has the thirty-seventh lowest incarceration rate in the world with 282 per 100,000 versus America, which has the highest incarceration rate in the world at 743 per 100,000—yes, much higher than China or Russia, who lack the equivalent of the prison industry lobby that exists in Washington. These are just a few of the disparities between the America's sick economy and a typical healthy economy like Taiwan's.

So why is Taiwan's economy so much more stable and prosperous than ours? The simple answer is, they simply have less corruption and greed in their government; but the more complex, but still very easy to understand, answer has to do with four basic economic fundamentals that America lacks but that are essential for any country that wants to be successful in today's global economy. They are the following: (1) The country must have a one-payer, government-run health-care system or its close equivalent. (2) The country's defense spending must be reduced to 10 percent of GDP. (3) The country must have a progressive tax rate, at least as high as the Clinton-era tax rates. (4) The country cannot have excessive influence of money and power in elections. There are eight other changes we should make here in America, and I will cover those in the subsequent chapter.

Now let me explain in dollars and cents how it would change America if it could implement these four simple policies. *First*, a one-payer, government-run universal health-care system has been shown to be many times better than a private insurance-run health-care system. But aside from the sheer benefit of having 100 percent of Americans covered with good health insurance, making for a much healthier population, the savings in dollars would be astronomical. It is simple mathematics; America would save something on the order of $1.25 trillion annually on health care if it would just copy Taiwan's progressive universal health-care system (the best in the world). Around $800 billion of those savings would go directly into the pockets of employers and consumers in lower health insurance premiums, and the other $400 billion would be saved by the federal government in lowered Medicare and Medicaid costs. *Second*, defense spending; America spends approximately seven times as much as China on defense, the superpower that spends the second most on defense, and when you think about it, China can actually afford to spend that much because they have so much liquidity whereas it is virtual insanity for us, who are essentially bankrupt, to be spending that kind of money on defense. If we cut our defense budget in half, we would still be spending three times as much as China. For a country that is basically bankrupt, that is enough. That would save almost $400 billion annually.

Third, we must return to the Clinton-era tax rates because we can't continue to spend ten or twenty times what other countries are spending on defense and two to three times what other countries are spending on health care per capita and still have one of the lowest effective tax rates in the developed world. Again, it is simple math: you can't spend ten times as much per capita as other countries and then take in less per capita in taxes and not run huge annual deficits.

But I really like what George Bush said when somebody questioned him about lowering taxes during a time when more revenues were needed, with two wars and the impending financial crisis coming. When the interviewer suggested that most economists didn't think it was good economic policy to reduce revenues when expenses were increasing. Mr. Bush replied something to the effect of "Well, I don't know what book on economics they read." Since most of the economists the interviewer was speaking about had actually written books on economics, and I am not sure George had ever actually read one, I am sure you can see the humor in the moment. I don't have any doubt that both George Bush and Dick Cheney fell asleep in their college economics class, which is just as well since I doubt that they would have understood the lectures if they had stayed awake. The bottom line is that the Bush tax cuts cost America approximately $700 billion annually or $7 trillion over a decade. The Afghanistan and Iraq wars have cost an estimated $5 trillion to $6 trillion. The repeal of mortgage and banking regulations and the dismantling of regulatory agencies, which resulted in the biggest financial collapse since the Great Depression, probably cost on the order of $5 trillion or $6 trillion. They also left a built-in infrastructure debt because they didn't keep up with repairing or building new infrastructure. I estimate that to be $3 trillion to $4 trillion. Total cost of the Bush/Cheney economic policies, probably in the range of $17 trillion to $25 trillion. Sorry to depress those voters who got hoodwinked into voting for those two little devils.

One other individual whom I think should shoulder a large part of the blame for the financial disaster that Bush and Cheney created is Alan Greenspan. An economist who apparently forgot everything he had ever been taught in school and who passively sat by without uttering a single word of objection when taxes were lowered to a degree that guaranteed massive annual federal deficits and while Wall Street, the banks, savings, and loans were deregulated, guaranteeing that these institutions would fall prey to massive amounts of corruption. He didn't exhibit any more economic common sense than a five-year-old as he watched and aided in the dismantling of the American economy (what a pinhead). *Fourth,* I've already covered the cost of the Bush tax cuts under defense spending because I wanted to give readers some estimate of the total economic damage caused by Bush, Cheney, and their buddy Alan Greenspan. But to review, it is almost $7 trillion over ten years. *Fifth,* There is also a huge cost to the Bush Supreme Court decision on *Citizens United* because now we waste astronomical amounts of money on campaigns, which could be used for other more useful purposes, and the money can come from any special interest group, even foreign ones, without disclosing the source. It has essentially finished the job the Bush Supreme Court set out to achieve, which was to take away the little bit of control citizens still had left of their own government and turn it over to corporations, the superrich, and special interests. The rest of that job is being done by the states and their Republican governors, who are restricting the voting rights of the poor, elderly, minorities, and students.

So let's imagine that our government wasn't totally corrupt for a minute and they would implement the same progressive, economically sound, and humane policies that societies like Taiwan, Germany, and the Netherlands have already done. Let see how much we, the taxpayers and business owners, would save over ten years: (1) If we would have implemented the same one-payer universal health-care system that Taiwan implemented in 1995, and it only took them three months, our federal government would have saved $4 trillion, and private citizens and businesses would have saved another $8 trillion. (2) If we would reduce our defense budget by half, the government would have saved $4 trillion. (3) If we would have maintained Clinton-era taxes, the government would have collected approximately an extra $7 trillion. (4) Reversing the *Citizens United* decision by the Supreme Court, I am sure, would save a good $4 trillion, which corporations could use to hire more employees and pay better benefits instead of using the money to corrupt our political system. So what does that all add up to? Approximately $10 trillion of savings over ten years for the federal government and almost $10 trillion worth of money put back into the pockets of private citizens and businesses and corporations. I also want to point out one other thing: you have to regulate Wall Street, the banks, savings, and loans despite what Eric Cantor and Paul Ryan say unless you are just begging for another financial meltdown and subsequent Great Depression.

So let me put all of this together for you in very simple terms: Our country already has a national debt of approximately $15 trillion. If we employ any of the budget proposals by Congressman Ryan, President Obama, or any of the current Republican candidates, we will see a federal debt climb to $20 trillion to $25 trillion or more inside the decade and still leave us with 9 percent unemployment or more, leave fifty million people without health care, see approximately the same poverty rate of 16 percent, see a million or so people still going bankrupt every year, see escalating education costs, see more disparity between rich and poor, little or no growth in GDP and Medicare, social security threatened, and voting would be restricted, which means they would not be fair. With my plan, we would pay off our federal debt in ten years, balance the annual budget, reduce unemployment to 3-4 percent; 100 percent of Americans would have good health insurance; the economy would grow by 4-8 percent every year; everybody who wanted it could afford secondary education; nobody would go bankrupt due to health-care costs; our elections would be fair; and everybody could vote.

Wouldn't it be wonderful to have a country like Taiwan, Singapore, or the Netherlands, with only 3 percent unemployment, 1 percent poverty, nobody without good health insurance, nobody going bankrupt due to health-care costs, a federal deficit of only 30 percent of GDP, an economy growing at 4-6 percent annually, no wars, modern infrastructure like bullet trains, inexpensive secondary education for our kids, and less disparity in wealth? Why wouldn't you want that? There are only three possible reasons: (1) you are a masochist, (2) you are somebody profiting from all the misery and you are so dysfunctional and greedy that you take pleasure in it, or (3) you simply don't understand enough about your government to vote in your own best interest.

The bottom line is this: if America doesn't adopt a one-payer, government-run universal health-care system like Taiwan's, reduce its defense budget in half, and go back to something similar to Clinton-era tax rates, we will never be a nation of equality and opportunity for all again. It is as simple as that, and don't let any of our boneheaded elected officials convince you otherwise.

Before you vote next time, ask yourself the following question: do I want to live in a country where 20 or 30 percent of its people live in poverty, with 10 or 15 percent unemployment, 20 to 30 percent of people without health insurance, and a staggering and destabilizing national debt, a country that massively overspends on defense and health care and doesn't tax the wealthy and powerful enough to pay for the massively expensive wars and private insurance-controlled health care that they voted for, a country that continues to fight wars of occupation; lets its most vulnerable, the elderly and children, live in poverty and insecurity; and redistributes wealth from the poorest to the most wealthy by under taxing investment earnings, the major income for the wealthy? A country whose economy is barely growing and isn't producing enough new jobs to keep up with new entries into the job market, routinely allows its politicians and powerful elite to rob the poor, doesn't believe in voting rights for all, and enacts laws to prevent the access to voting?

If you don't want the country to keep going down this road, then you have to demand more from the government and stop voting for obviously corrupt politicians. How do you do that? It is not so difficult. Just keep in mind that this nation had its best years, by far, when it had adequate regulation of the banks, Wall Street, and savings and loans; when taxes were fair and didn't redistribute wealth from the poor and middle class to the richest 1 percent. Those years were the Franklin Delano Roosevelt, Dwight D. Eisenhower, William Jefferson Clinton, and yes, Jimmy Carter years when taxes on the highest earners were somewhere between 39 and 90 percent. Yes, despite those higher levels of taxes on the wealthy, they still continued to become incredibly wealthier. Remember, FDR finished with something like an 80 percent approval rating at the end of his administration, and Eisenhower had about a 60 percent approval rating when he left office. Clinton is, of course, one of the most popular presidents ever post presidency. Presently, legislation enacted during the Bush administration has the wealthy only paying about 15 percent because most of their income comes from investment. Yet these same individuals who are paying virtually no taxes relative to their income are the very individuals that voted for extravagant wars and defense budgets and insisted on maintaining the most inefficient, most expensive, and most abusive medical system in the developed world while, at the same time, funding corrupt politicians—like Phil Graham and John McCain in the past and currently Eric Cantor and Paul Ryan—to enact legislation to deregulate banks and Wall Street so these institutions can continue to bring down financial markets as a result of unregulated speculation and gambling on markets and then send the bill to you, your children, and your grandchildren.

So at the present, I would not vote for a single Republican or Blue Dog Democrat, and even though, at the present, the Democratic Party is the most reasonable party to vote for, even they need to have their feet held to the fire by the voting public. They should be voted out of office the minute they don't support legislation to enact universal health care; a 50 percent reduction of the defense budget; and a much, much more progressive tax code. They should also be willing to keep pushing to reverse the *Citizens United* decision that was enacted by our present Supreme Court, the most corrupt American Supreme Court in fifty years. We should all support labor, Occupy Wall Street, and a free press. These are the policies that will establish America as a humane and prosperous society again. I truly believe that if these steps aren't taken, America will never recover its prominent place in the world or provide a hopeful future for coming generations for working-class Americans.

Let me put it in terms of dollars and cents. Imagine our budget in terms of single dollar bills instead of trillions of dollars. When Bush and Cheney came into office, the government was taking in revenues of a little over $2 annually, and it was spending about $2, leaving a little left over to continue to pay down America's total debt, which at the time was about $5. Now comes the infamous team of Bush and (Debt Doesn't Matter) Cheney and their gaggle of oddball neocons. What did they do to the budget? First, they lowered taxes on everybody, but most significantly on their rich buddies, which cost America about 70¢ annually, immediately causing us to start running deficits instead of slight surpluses. Incredibly stupid, you say? And if you said that, you would be absolutely right. So the last thing on earth any government would want to do, once they had already established a significant annual debt with your tax policies, is start spending more; only a complete idiot would do that, right? Yes, you're right, and that's exactly what George and Dick decided to do. Now sometimes you can spend or invest in things that will eventually create revenues, like creating new infrastructure that makes transportation more efficient or education that creates a more productive and marketable workforce, but what you absolutely don't want to do is start a war, especially one of occupation (which General Eisenhower, the commander of the Allied forces in World War II and one of our best presidents ever, said would be a very stupid thing to do). So of course, you could already guess that George and Dick went ahead and started two unfunded wars of occupation. You would have to be the two worst and stupidest politicians in history to do that, wouldn't you?

Yes, absolutely, no doubts of any kind; they get the award. They started two unfunded wars costing another 50¢ a year. Now we are running a $1.20 deficit every year instead of breaking even. Then they enacted an unfunded drug supplement package, the Medicare supplement D package that added another 25¢ annually to the budget. So now we are at a deficit of $1.45 annually. The final thing the dynamic duo did was make sure markets were unregulated and regulatory agencies weren't given enough funding or personnel to properly regulate, which resulted in the biggest financial collapse since the Great Depression. That will cost at least 50¢ annually for perpetuity. So the total damage caused by the dynamic duo is about $2 annually of built-in deficits.

Let's not forget the dysfunctional and unfair division of wealth that exists in our country because of thirty years or so of the neocon policies of Reagan, Bush, and Cheney. In America, which has the worst disparity in wealth in the developed world, 10 percent of Americans own 75 percent of America's wealth, and unbelievably, 1 percent of Americans control 40 percent of America's wealth. Now get that straight in your head: 1 percent, a tiny little fraction of the nation's population, owns almost 50 percent of the nation's wealth. So let's imagine a society where there is only $100 of wealth to split up among one hundred people each day. So whatever each person gets of that $100 is their total budget for the day. If you split up the $100 each day in the same way wealth is split up in America, it would mean one very greedy person would get $40 each day and the other ninety-nine people would receive about 60¢. But the situation in America is really worse than that because the top 10 percent owns 75 percent of the wealth of the nation. So, after the top 1 percent takes their 40 percent share, the next 9 percent will split up 35 percent of the wealth, leaving the remaining 90 percent to split up 25 percent of the wealth. Thus, in my hypothetical society, that would mean one person would get $40 per day, nine people would get about $4 per day, and the remaining ninety people would get about 27¢ per day, about one-two hundredths of what the greedy 1 percent gets to live on each day. But it is even worse than that because the 1-10 percent, in addition to the disparity of income, also own most of all land, businesses, and property, and with our present tax structure, that wealth disparity will just continue to get worse, if you can imagine that, in the next decade.

I might also add that any nation that used the America's neocon model as a blueprint to plan their own society has experienced exactly the same problems of inequality, unemployment, excessive cost of education, and human disparity. Israel, for example, has a similar economic structure, and in a nation of about eight million people, twenty-seven families control almost 50 percent of the total wealth of the nation, and of course, the neocons there are exactly like the neocons in America. They have learned to use the media and label anyone who would suggest changing the system so it would be more equal as being unpatriotic, socialist, communist, or just plain unchristian.

WHY UNIVERSAL HEALTH

As you may or may not know, the World Health Organization (WHO) rates health-care systems. *Singapore*, which is rated number 6 on the WHO chart, only spends 4 percent of its GDP on their form of universal health care.

Taiwan—which is not on the WHO chart because it is considered to be part of China; however, it has its own independent health-care system, which many experts believe to be the best health-care system in the world—spends less than 8 percent of its GDP on health care and has a one-payer, government-administered universal health-care system. They are also becoming a very popular destination for medical tourism, Exceeding 100 thousand visitors annually.

So what is Taiwan and Singapore getting for their health-care dollars that the United States isn't? And does the money they save on health care give them, and all countries with well-developed universal health-care systems, an insurmountable advantage in the global economy? The answer is yes.

Universal Health Care versus America's Health-Care System

1. In Taiwan, and all universal health-care countries, 100 percent of the population is covered with good quality health-care insurance, whereas in America, only about 80 percent are covered by health-care insurance; and of those, only half have good-quality health-care insurance, which leaves 150 million people, half our population, with inadequate or no health-care insurance. Fifty million people are completely uninsured in America.
2. In universal health-care countries, nobody dies because they don't have access to health care, whereas in America, over fifty thousand

people die needlessly every year because they lack access to health care, which is the equivalent to the number of American deaths that occurred in the eight years of the Vietnam War, every single year. Just think, in an eight-year period, four hundred thousand people will die needlessly in America, eight times the number of Americans that died in the Vietnam War. Is that really what you want to happen in America?

3. Nobody goes bankrupt in universal health-care countries because of health-care costs, whereas in America, one million people and families go bankrupt every single year, and ten million every decade, because of health-care costs. Unbelievably, 45 percent of those who go bankrupt in America actually have health insurance (this shows how inadequate most health-care insurance is in America).

4. Studies show that people in universal health-care countries live longer and are happier.

5. When surveyed, people who live in countries with universal health care are much more satisfied with their health-care systems than we Americans are with ours.

6. There is less infant mortality in countries with universal health care because there is better overall prenatal care.

7. When surveyed, virtually 100 percent of respondents who presently live in countries with well-established universal health-care systems emphatically rejected the thought of replacing their system with an American-like health-care system.

8. The man who was voted the most important figure in Canadian History by an overwhelming majority of Canadians is Tommy Douglas, the Father of Universal Health Care in Canada. Do you think Rick Scott, former CEO of the Columbia Hospital Corporation (the largest hospital corporation in America at the time) and now a billionaire and the governor of Florida, would be voted an important historical figure in America? I think he would be much more likely to be voted one of the most nefarious figures in American history.

Now let's look at the financial advantages of universal health care; they are gargantuan, and they give any country that has a well-developed universal health-care system a huge advantage in the global economy.

Let's compare Taiwan's health-care costs to America's health-care costs. This is comparing the costs associated with what many experts rate as the number one health-care system in the developed world, Taiwan's, to the costs of the health-care system rated by the World Health Organization as the worst health-care system in the developed world (number 38), America's:

1. Taiwan spends only 8 percent of its GDP on health care, and that percentage of expenditure is fairly stable and not increasing significantly over time. America spends about 17.5 percent of its GDP on health care, and that percentage is increasing rapidly over time. The math is simple: if America would adopt Taiwan's efficient form of health care, it would save about $1.25 trillion annually (that is equivalent to saving $3,000 annually for every man, woman, and child in America or $30,000 for every man, woman, and child every decade). If you multiply that savings by the three hundred million people who live in America, that is about $10 trillion every 10 years; it actually ends up being about $12 trillion or $13 trillion. Presently, our total debt after about 240 years of being a nation is, approximately, a crippling $15 trillion; however, it would be only $2 trillion if it hadn't been for the extravagant spending of the Reagan and Bush Jr. administrations. Two-thirds of the savings from universal health care over 10 years. If we had Taiwan's system of universal health care, about $7 trillion would go back into the pockets of the American people and businessmen. Three to four trillion dollars would go back into the US Treasury as savings from the reduced cost of Medicare, Medicaid, and veterans' benefits
2. Do you begin to see the impact of America's excessive spending on health care? So every year, about $800 billion of savings

would be put back into the private sector by reducing the cost of insurance premiums to both businesses and private citizens and co-pays to private citizens.
3. The annual savings for the federal government would be about $400 billion in the form of reduced Medicare, Medicaid, and retired veterans' benefits costs.
4. It has been estimated that implementing universal health care and the resultant savings to American car manufacturers would reduce the manufacturing cost of an American car by $1,500 to $2,000, which could be passed on as savings to the consumer, and that same effect would be felt across the board by all American manufacturers and, as a result, would immediately create millions of new American manufacturing jobs because of the increased competitiveness of American manufacturers, not to mention the huge increase in medical tourism dollars and jobs that an improved and more economical health-care industry would create.
5. It is also very important to note that Taiwan implemented their universal health-care system in just three months. It is so efficient, it is even easy to implement.

Now let's look at why Taiwan's universal health care is so much more efficient and less expensive than America's private insurance-controlled health-care system; the reasons are simple and easy to understand:

1. In Taiwan, everybody contributes to the pool of money supporting universal health care. Yes, I know what you are thinking, and you are right—it's an individual mandate. No insurance system works without a mandate for everybody to participate. We all have to purchase car insurance in order to drive, even if we never get in an accident. We agree to do that because the government mandates it for the common good so that a car accident doesn't bankrupt each individual who is unlucky enough to get in one; otherwise, only incredibly rich people like Mitt Romney and George W. Bush could afford to drive.

2. Because there is only one insurance company in Taiwan, which is administered by the government, it is simple, efficient, and cheap. Taiwan only spends 2 percent of its health-care dollars for administration, whereas America spends at least 25 percent, wasting something like $400 billion annually in just pure administrative inefficiency. Any country that would waste that much money every year with no return on their investment is unbelievably stupid, wouldn't you agree?
3. The efficiency and reduced cost in Taiwan's health-care system results in less patient hassle, more convenience, and as a result, better diagnoses. When you are registered into the national health-care system in Taiwan, you get a smart card that has all your information and medical history; no more filling out a new medical history every time you visit the doctor. The doctor or nurse simply scans your smart card, and all your information is available in seconds to the doctor or nurse, no paperwork. The doctor does the exam and whatever procedures they need to do, and when the appointment is over, they or their nurse simply scans a bar code from a menu of bar codes for each procedure, and it is automatically billed electronically to the government run insurance company; no paperwork for you, just a nominal co-pay.
4. In addition, most of the time, no appointment is needed; you can go directly to the generalist or specialist of your choice.

Now, why wouldn't every American want an economical, guaranteed quality health-care system like Taiwan's that is convenient and hassle-free? There is one reason and one reason only. Americans have been brainwashed by Fox News, the Koch brothers, and corrupt politicians into thinking it is un-American to want good things for themselves and their children if it in any way reduces the massive bonuses, salaries, golden-umbrella retirement plans, and profits paid to the greediest CEOs and companies in American history. Who make on average three hundred times what the average American worker makes. You know, the Job Creators! Let me break down for you where the extra $1.25 trillion you are spending on health care in excess of what you would be spending in Taiwan goes, and you tell me if it is a good value.

First, you are spending approximately $200 billion to $300 billion annually for inflated salaries, bonuses, and golden-umbrella retirement packages to ensure the disgustingly opulent lives of American health-care company CEOs and their families (remember, about thirty years ago, CEOs only made about thirty times what the average worker makes, and they were more than happy with that). Not today's new greedier brand of CEO, like Rick Scott, now governor of Florida. These guys are even greedier than the robber barons of the gilded age. Second, you are spending $200 billion to $300 billion annually in wasted administrative costs because private insurance-controlled health-care systems are inherently much more wasteful and inefficient than universal health-care systems. Third, you are being massively overbilled for health insurance and co-pays by at least $800 billion. Yes, that adds up to approximately $1.25 trillion annually that you pay extra for the privilege of having the worst health-care system in the developed world. Is it worth it? Is this what you really want?

Well, here is a short list of people who want you and your children to be stuck with the present horrible system of health care: Rush Limbaugh; Bill O'Reilly; Shawn Hannity; Ann Coulter; Rupert Murdoch; Fox News; the Koch brothers; Eric Cantor; Mitch McConnell; Newt Gingrich; the Tea Party; the Heritage Foundation; Justice Clarence Thomas and his wife; Justice Antonio Scalia; Justice John Roberts; Justice Samuel Alito; John Boehner; Phil Graham and his wife; Herman Cain; all CEOs of hospital, pharmacy, and insurance corporations; the AMA; CEOs of the banks; CEOs of Wall Street; hedge fund managers; Larry Summers; and Grover Norquist. These people and institutions are so greedy, they make Ebenezer Scrooge seem like Mother Teresa and the Grim Reaper like the angel of mercy. What is amazing to me is that even President Obama got conned into stumping and lobbying for the powerful insurance, hospital, and pharmacy corporations and advocated maintaining America's present miserable and economically crippling form of health care. He made, what

I think, is one of the most ignorant and destructive statements in American political history, essentially saying that Universal healthcare is not right for America. Yes, why would Americans want to have a system that would provide many times better health care at half the price and ten times the convenience? Crazy, what could they be thinking? The problem is that Fox News, our incredibly corrupt bought politicians, right-wing think tanks (like the Heritage Foundation), a right-wing Supreme Court, and our unbelievably spineless Democratic politicians who don't stand for anything and back down anytime they are challenged (like the Blue Dog Democrats) have done a great job of convincing the average working American that it is unpatriotic and unchristian to vote against the 1 percent (who now owns 40 percent of all wealth in America); and likewise, that it is unpatriotic and unchristian to vote in their own best interest and for the well-being of their own children and fellow workers. Yes, voting against the 1 percent constitutes "class warfare," but fleecing the US Treasury out of an excess of $10 trillion to $15 trillion, leaving the American taxpayer with a multigenerational debt, massive unemployment, loss of millions of homes, loss of many people's retirement benefits, unaffordable educational costs, and tens of millions of people without health care is just good old patriotic American ingenuity.

Any country that wants to join the modern world, be competitive on world markets, become a humane and prosperous country with low unemployment, have 8-10 percent annual GDP growth, have nonexistent poverty rates, have economically stable safety net programs (social security, Medicare, and Medicaid), have low-cost secondary education, have students that rate academically in the top ten countries in the world in math and science, have adequate money for replacing existing infrastructure and for building new modern infrastructure (like bullet trains), reduce its health-care cost to 8 percent or less relative to GDP, elevate its quality of health care to become one of the top ten health-care providers in the world based on WHO ratings, and attract large amounts of medical tourism dollars will need to convert to a one-payer universal health-care system like Taiwan's. There is not another good alternative.

There are of course other things America must do to fix the massive damage caused by the Bush/Cheney administration and, to a lesser degree, by Reagan, and they would include the following:

1. Reduce defense spending to 10 percent of GDP down from 20 percent.
2. Return to at least the Clinton-era taxes for everybody, but really, the top tax rate should be at least 40 percent.
3. Establish a really good recycling system like Germany's.
4. Reverse the *Citizens United* decision by the Supreme Court.
5. Make sure we establish strong laws to regulate financial markets and enforce those laws so we avoid more financial crises, which all occurred because of deregulation.
6. We must extend the payroll tax to the first $200,000 of income, not just the $106,000.
7. Capital gains should be taxed at the same rate as income past the first $100,000 unless the person is a broker or a hedge fund manager, in which case it should all be taxed as regular income.
8. Derivatives or swap transactions should be taxed at a quarter of a percent.
9. Social security should be means tested as a way of keeping it solvent along with extending the payroll tax.
10. We also need to outlaw the credit default swap (CDS), which is essentially an illegal bet on the market that only brokers with inside information and their clients benefit from and that nobody in their right minds and who wasn't a completely corrupt Wall Street banker, broker, or politician would allow.

These ten simple steps, changes in our economic policies, would rapidly convert our country from one that is acquiring debt at the rate of about $1 trillion annually; that has a 16 to 20 percent rate of poverty; that is overspending its defense budget by $400 billion annually; that is overspending on health care by $1.25 trillion annually between the government and the private sector and not getting a thing for the money;

that has an incarceration rate ten to twenty times of other developed countries; whose students only rank twentieth or twenty-fifth in the world in math and science because secondary education costs are the highest in the developed world; whose unemployment rate is a perpetual 10 percent or above; whose economic growth is stagnant; whose infrastructure, roads, bridges, sewers, electrical grids, and public water systems are all decaying; whose political system is so completely corrupted it no longer functions on behalf of the populace but is completely controlled by a few special interests; that has the greatest disparity between rich and poor in the developed world; where fifty million people have no health insurance and fifty thousand people die needlessly every year because they lack access to health care; and where one million people go bankrupt every year because of excessive health-care expenses, to a country that has an annual budget surpluses; that has 10 percent or less military spending; that has low unemployment of 3-4 percent; that has virtually no poverty; that has very inexpensive secondary education and, as a result, students who rank first or second in math and science; that has a consistent increase of 4-8 percent of GDP annually in economic growth; that has a well-funded and secure social safety net (social security, Medicare, Medicaid, and veterans' benefits); that has the money to invest in new infrastructure (bullet trains) and to replace old infrastructure; and whose government is functioning properly (making rational decisions) on behalf of the people, not special interests and those with excessive influence. I am talking about countries like Taiwan, the Netherlands, Singapore, Germany, Austria, Switzerland, Norway, Denmark, and to a degree, Canada.

MY PERSONAL EXPERIENCE AS A PATIENT WITH THE AMERICAN HEALTH-CARE SYSTEM

I am going to use my story as a typical example of a patient using the American health-care system because I think my story is similar to those of the million people who go bankrupt each year in America due to illness and the fifty thousand people who die every year in America because they are ill and have no health insurance. If you think about these statistics in a little more depth, you can see the moral issue America faces regarding health care. If we keep the same or similar health-care system for the next decade, we as a people will be responsible for ten million families going bankrupt and five hundred thousand needless deaths; that is a lot to bear morally, especially since the solution is so simple. Another way of putting it is that we could have the best health-care system in the world, cover everybody, prevent one million bankruptcies a year, prevent fifty thousand needless deaths every year, and save $1 trillion a year. If we are not smart enough to switch to a system of universal health care like Taiwan's, then I suppose we deserve what we get.

Before I tell my story as a patient, let me first relate a few observations—remember, these are generalizations, and of course, there are exceptions—about doctors in America.

First, a general statistic: when you see a doctor in America, some studies have shown that you have only a one in three chance of being diagnosed correctly, and of course, your chances become exponentially worse if your disease is rare or difficult to diagnose.

What could be the problem? Let's do a little diagnosis of our own. If the disease is a dysfunctional behavior of doctors in America, what is the underlying cause? I think it is safe to say, to a large degree, that it is the control of doctors in America by the private insurance industry. I say that because I have observed many doctors in my thirty years as a patient, and almost without fail and with few exceptions, they make these fatal mistakes: (1) Failure to carefully heed the patient's medical history, often expressing skepticism or dismissing the patient history altogether, in essence, making up the patient's history for them so it fits into a preconceived diagnosis. They would do much better to accept the patient's history as the patient relates it but leave it open to change by the patient as the patient remembers more. (2) Failure to do a differential diagnosis is an extremely common mistake made by physicians in America, and it is the major cause of the next fatal mistake, which is treating the symptoms rather than determining the underlying cause. Without doing a differential, there is often little chance of making the right diagnosis of many common diseases but certainly of any difficult or rare disease. (3) The reason treating symptoms is so popular among American physicians is because it takes so much less time than determining the underlying cause, and in many clinics, doctors are pressured to see as many patients as possible during a workday. (4) Doctors letting their egos get in the way of good medicine, which leads to a certain rigidness in behavior, making it difficult to just say "I don't know," to make good referrals, and to listen respectfully to the patient. (5) Lack of curiosity and simply becoming jaded because of the system. Yes, doctors are also being abused by the system set up by private insurance companies. Doctors are only human, and they too become emotionally fatigued by the constant hassles and financial and administrative hurdles set up by private insurance companies.

We as patients make mistakes regarding our own health care, which contribute to the problem, and I have made every one of the mistakes I will mention next. The first mistake we make is to trust the system too completely. Be protective of yourself; if you have been seeing a doctor for a significant period of time, and the treatment he is providing isn't improving your symptoms or you're actually becoming more symptomatic, think about seeing somebody else (isn't doing the same thing over and over again and getting the same bad result the definition of insanity?). If you're unable to talk with your doctor and act as a partner in your own health care, then look for a new doctor. If your doctor is condescending or egotistical, get a new doctor. Take the time if you can to become educated about your own symptoms and diseases; the Internet is a very powerful tool, and if you have the right doctor, as I do now, you can be an invaluable resource to them in determining a diagnosis and treatment. In many cases, you can become the most knowledgeable expert about your own disease, and that is a very gratifying experience. Oh yes, and sometimes it takes a little courage to say no to a physician or to demand that you be a partner in your own health care.

As a prelude to using my case as an example of how the American health-care system works, I want to lay the groundwork by noting some general facts about my case. I have the following conditions: limited Wegener's granulomatosis, dermatomyositis, and celiac sprue disease,. These would all be serious conditions individually, but together if they go untreated for decades, as mine did, they are nothing short of a nightmare symptomatically speaking. I could have been diagnosed as early as age twenty-seven because I already had the classic initial symptom of Wegener's disease, which was chronic rhinosinusitis untreatable by conventional means, and my family history was that my father had exactly the same thing. Unfortunately, I wasn't diagnosed until I was fifty-six, and the diagnosis was not made by my doctors but by me using the Internet and the generous help of my general practitioner (Mark Bjorklund), who ordered lab tests, imaging studies, and took biopsies I needed to make a definitive diagnosis. Ultimately, I got my diagnosis confirmed by a noted dermatologist (Dr. David Carey) and a nationally known rheumatologist (Dr. Mark Cohen). A note about Dr. Bjorklund: without him I never would have been able to make such a specific diagnosis. He agreed to be my partner in determining the underlying cause of my symptoms and did it without letting his ego get in the way. He even told me that I was the only patient he ever had that knew more about my own disease than he did. He also told me that working with me gave him a new perspective when seeing his other patients and that he pays much more attention to his patient's history and what his patient is telling him. To me, Mark is the ideal general practitioner and what every patient should be looking for.

During the years between twenty-six and fifty-six, my symptoms slowly became worse until they were disabling and nothing short of a human nightmare. I ultimately lost almost everything that was important to me in life, before I was diagnosed and treated, including: my marriage, home, profession, friends, savings, retirement accounts, any semblance of a normal life, my disability insurance (disability insurance companies don't pay for disability unless there is a diagnosis, and my doctors had none), and a healthy appendix and gall bladder due to misdiagnosis; and because I had long term malabsorption syndrome due to untreated celiac sprue disease, I also had a B12 deficiency that caused dementia, short- and long-term memory loss, and depression. So in a sense, I lost my sanity. I was also in debt up to my ears and exhausted beyond anything I ever imagined; I truly was not doing well. All of this personal tragedy I have described was caused more by our dysfunctional health-care system than by my diseases because my diseases were easily diagnosable and treatable.

www.ingramcontent.com/pod-product-compliance
Lightning Source LLC
Chambersburg PA
CBHW021047180526
45163CB00005B/2313